Swords, Shields, & Hospital Gowns

Amelia Blackwater

Cover Design by Amelia Blackwater

Contact: ablackwaterpoetry@gmail.com
IG: @ameliablackwater
TikTok: @ameliablackwater

Trigger Warning

Please practice self-care before, while, and after reading.

Poetry contains
- *Mental illness and ableism*
- *Self-harm and suicide*
- *Eating disorders and body hatred*
- *Sexual Assault and rape*
- *Emotional and Physical Abuse*
- *Death or dying*
- *Sexism and misogyny*
- *And more*

My poetry has been my therapy. I hope that my story might help you realize that you are not alone. These poems have been a way to relieve the pain, to share my story and to hopefully help others through their pain.
We are warriors, survivors, and all-around bad asses.

Dedication

To my soul mate, Daniel. You have always believed in me and guided me through this journey. You have helped make me this strong independent feminist woman. I would not be here today if it wasn't for you. I love you.

Table of Contents

Prologue

All my life everyone has wanted me to sugar coat my writings. Add a dash of rainbows and shitting sunflower daisies, I don't fucking know, It's not my style. I'm not here to brighten your day and make you feel like you just ran through a field of daffodils on a bright summer day. All I can hope is that there is someone out there who will connect through the words. Feel release through mutual pain, realize you aren't the only one. My story is a long one. Which is crazy, for a girl who has so far only lived thirty years. Believe me, it sounds absurd to me too. I was born complicated. On that day I already had a story to tell. The story kept building from then on, beautiful and tragic, and writing it was the only thing that got me where I am today, alive.

Part I

Scars

Some of us are born new,
some are born with complications
but we all leave this world with scars.

Invisible Warriors

You are not invisible,
your story is full of
strength & courage
you don't owe anyone
an explanation
screw apologies,
you are a warrior,
glorious & proud!

Notes from a Rag Doll

I was born a torn-up piece of shit, a broken doll that had to be fixed.
I was never new.
Sometimes, I believe what I was born into, all lead up to this.
My mental disorders only mask the scars original to this body.
When I got older, I started to read more about my nature.
I could read shit tons of books about things I thought was wrong
with me.
I would find myself in the pages.
I would think to myself, "this is so me."
As if I was reading a horoscope instead of a description about a
mental disorder.
Now, I wish I had never subjected myself to reading them,
because I can no longer tell if I've just become a hypochondriac or
if I'm just really that screwed up. Depending on the day, depends on
my view.
Maybe, if I could just go back to being the kid with a heart problem.
But it was,
I was,
never that simple.

Rag Doll

I am a poor rag doll
sewn too quickly back together.
My chest is stitched,
my threads ache,
keep the stuffing in,
but the scar still lingers

I am Frankenstein's monster.
I was born to be other men's experiments
my vulnerabilities
left open for the world
to examine.

I'm a rag doll,
I'm the monster
you have created,
the discarded useless toy,
the failed science experiment.

Transposition of the Great Arteries

The anatomy of my heart
is a study of its own
one with a whole team
of doctors trying to piece back
this puzzle of a humpty dumpty,
my heart is like a freeway
with wrong turns and exits
that leads you through a loop,
but my heart heals and forgives
& it learns to march to its own beat.

A Simple Explanation to a Complex Problem

What exactly is wrong with your heart again?
It works backwards
like the way you think
it is okay to easily dismiss my illness
because it is invisible to your eyes
this is not the first time I have told you
& it will not be the last
listen with your ears
& not your eyes.

The Transformation

The heart breathes in palpitating rhythms,
murmurs of innocence lost
in hospital gowns & IV drips.
A silent yearning for the reaper to come
to this somber hospital bed,
where its skeleton cage holds her tight
& rocks her to sleep each night.

She prays that this night will be her last,
that her eyes will no longer fall upon
haggard faces of forgetful nurses
& sleepless parents.

The hospital walls are stark
like her personality
stripped cleaned with Clorox bleach
& morphine drips.
A Collapsed lung, issues repetitive screaming
from a machine telling her
to breathe deeper.
But the air isn't the same
she has been reborn
inhuman, unable to sustain life.

A Letter to Myself When in Hospital Beds

I'm not here to tell you that everything is going to be okay.
You got dealt a shit card &
It's fucking okay, not to be okay.
Don't feel guilty
It's not your fault you are sick
It is okay to be human
use your pain & experiences
to make something more.

A Slow Dance in Hospital Beds

We slow dance to
the sweet murmurs of
the hospital monitors
but it's so hard to
keep in time
with the off rhyme
of the hearts
tachycardic beats.

Anesthesia

When I fall asleep
where do I go
for I'm a restless one
there have been many
before me
who have fallen into
the deep slumber
for I'm a restless one
& I don't sleep much.

Side Effects

May Cause:
Insomnia
Anxiety
Depression
Mood Swings
          Out of Body Experiences

Hot Flashes
Loss of Period
Weight Loss
Weight Gain
          Spontaneous Combustion

Migraines
Bone Loss
Joint Pain
Backache
          Demonic Possession

Sticks & Stones

I dread laying down
the bones feel foreign to my body
They never seem to settle
Instead they play sticks & stones
Between ribs & bones
And pretend that each movement
doesn't hurt me.

Therapy

*Can someone explain to me
the fine line between
complaining,
venting,
& keeping it all inside*

Sympathy

*I never talk about my past for fear of evoking
sympathetic glances
static conversation is better than
haunting silence,
long awkward pauses
between
well wishes.*

*My mother stands around for hours
& talks to people we barely know
about my surgery,
as if I'm not standing in front of them,
then scolds me
for being rude & saying,
I don't want to talk about it.
I retort that she is being selfish,
pathetic in her attempt for sympathy.*

*I'm not the hero in this story
& I don't need your sympathy.*

Actions Speak Louder than Words

I carry a noose in my back pocket
I tend to hang myself with words.
Every day starts out the same,
everyday ends the same way too
maybe this day will be different.

So, I carry a noose in my back pocket
just in case I decide to hang myself today.
Letters form words
& words form a sentence,
in which I stutter upon saying.

I carry a noose in my back pocket,
I tend to hang myself with words,
so, I'll keep my mouth shut.

Actions speak louder than words.

Elephant in the Room

I got quiet.
I was scared that if I spoke too much about my illness,
complained a bit too much,
my identity would disappear
all that would be left
is a body with a heart
that doesn't work properly.
I would no longer be asked about my passions
the topic would be,
"How are you feeling?"
"Is everything okay?"
Most of the time it wasn't
but people don't want to hear that,
they don't know how to respond.
So, I smiled,
said fine & hope the subject changed.

Things to Not Say to Someone Who is Sick

10) Let me know what I can do to help
9) No really, I wish I could do something
8) Insert some new age remedy here that is completely unhelpful
7) You know everything happens for a reason & God doesn't give you more than what you can handle
6) You look terrible! Maybe if you get up & put on some clothes & makeup, you'll feel better.
5) You can beat this; it's going to be okay.
4) I am so sorry.
3) Don't you think are being over dramatic. You should get over it by now.
2) But you don't look sick.
1) Silence.

Different

As a child I was proud of my
long scar from my clavicle
to my navel till,
the other kids on the playground
pointed & told me that it meant
that I was different from them.

The Broken Hearted

They say hearts can be broken
Mended
Fixed
stitched
& healed
But the scars are forever there.
If we talk about love this way
Then why do we assume the
Anatomy is something different?
That if I am born with a broken heart
That it can be mended
& magically the damage was never done
That I am healed & the scars were
Never there?
A Congenital Heart defect
Does not just go away
There is still scar tissue left over
From years of abuse
Complications can still arise
Years after the heart
Has been left untouched.

Scars Pt I

The temporary stiff ache
of a stale body,
from weeks spent in the hospital
linger like the foul stench of
decomposing trash.
But the scars that are left
in the wake of the war
are what lasts.

The scars open the world to view
they invite people in
as point & ask questions
you aren't quite ready to reveal.
But the scars tell the story for you.

Reborn

The act of bathing seems
> *violent.*
The naked flesh
against the extreme temperatures.
> *Cold.*
Hot.
> *Cold.*
It seems to destroy my body
each morning as the
harsh water pulls at
> *my skin*
forces me into the brutal
> *bitter*
>> *air*
makes my body renewed,
> *reborn.*

What is the Appropriate Response when a Doctor Asks…?

"I'm Fine."
Is how I assume a normal person is supposed to respond
when someone asks,
"How you are doing?"

Upon Meeting my Doctor for the Second Time

I do not know you sir
but it seems that upon you
studying my file for
a couple minutes,
you want to search inside me
& heal me with the
hands of your God-like complex.

Homeless

My nails are dirty & jagged,
my bones are easily broken,
I'm not as intriguing,
as people say.
For I fear,
all that was once beautiful
in my body & soul,
has left me to go find another,
& all hope that I had,
left & never came back.

Attention Whore

*I cannot control
the rhythm of my heart
it is loud as it palpitates
in the veins of my neck
begging for attention.
Look at it! My scar
is fresh for the world to see.
I resent the anatomy within
this body. The attention it craves.
The control it has.*

And the Oscar goes to…

I don't want to be that
kind of woman who
parades their illness/crazy
like a gold medal
that everyone should applaud
her for. Like she has just won the fucking
Oscar for her performance &
the audience should give her a standing ovation.

Count Back from Ten...

The cut of a scalpel changes you.
How many times has the deep sleep of anesthesia
forever changed my identity?
How many different people could I have been?
Those women,
are collected deep inside my subconscious
loss potential mixed with
faded memories of a girl who used to be
so different.

Fears

I'm not afraid of death.
I have met him before in cold hospital beds.
I'm afraid of lost time & sympathetic glances
of fighting with insurances & doctors
I'm terrified that all I'll be remembered for
are chaos & hospital bills.

An Open Letter to My Insurance Company

To whom it may concern,
May I ask,
Who should pay for my medical bills?
For a disease I was born with
I'm not that innocent child on a poster
From the American Heart association anymore,
I'm a grown ass woman
A success story with challenges.
Because of this, I know you believe that I don't quite
Deserve the care that the children do
But my health matters.
I know that I cost you more than
What you believe my life is worth.
Some crazy math has determined that if you
Make it absolutely impossible to get the care I need
Then maybe I will give up.
Well in case you were wondering
I am not giving up.

Part II

The Body

I've spent years of my life in front of the mirror

denying myself the nourishment

to sustain this life

(I am hungry no longer)

Demons

There are demons
hiding in these bones
waiting to be released.

A History of Eating

Looking back, I wonder
did I ever feel comfortable in my body?
It always felt heavy
food was foreign in my stomach
even when I was a child I would
often throw away my lunches
because I wanted more time
to play, & earthly needs like
eating, bathing, sleeping was time consuming
& there was always something better to do.

Hungry

*I'm waiting for
my ribs to emerge
from my body
cut the flesh & strip
away the sin.
The skeleton within
hollow and marrow
as my soul
creeps out
of my
skin.*

The Easiest Lie I Ever Told

Not hungry.

Odd Girl Out

How to not be the odd girl
because if you are the unusual
nerdy, geek, know-it-all,
you are mocked, pointed at, criticized
you start to harbor the guilt within
because you are not like the other girls
you aren't skinny enough,
you haven't learned how to paint your face with
the correct colors & contours,
your imperfections are at the front lines
& you would start a war if it meant that it would
attract the allies to your side &
you would no longer be
the odd girl.

Lunches

Whenever I would push
my lunch tray in his direction
his mouth would turn up
& smile
he loved the extra chocolate milk
in my naivety I thought,
as my waist shrank
his love for me
would grow.

I Win

We compared scars
in the firelight
counting who had more
whose were deeper
as if it was some twisted competition
where the sickest person wins the trophy.

Daily Devotions Pt 1

Tips, tricks & goal weights
I cut out magazines &
hang thinspiration quotes on my fridge
like they are the gospel,
my daily devotion,
pray to disappear &
deny myself to be holy.

Anxiety

I feel like a song
that has a bridge
with no chorus;
like a story
with a climax
& no ending;
Like the night before
the battle
restless & war hungry.

Calories & Scars

I wanted to be perfect for him
the way he had to be perfect
for himself.
I wanted our bones to fit like puzzle pieces,
the perfect fit.
But my destruction never was his
drug of choice
& no one was willing
to be the stronger person
for the other
We were too wrapped up in comparing
calories & scars.

Empty Soul

*I'm terrified of this silence
& the meaning behind
our deaf ears.
Dead weather,
leads to a stagnate life.
I'm no longer the girl you seek,
behind cold eyes
lies empty souls.*

Depression, I Will Win This Fight

I can't breathe
I feel like a demon
has its hands around my neck
choking away my sanity,
right before I can't take it anymore,
when life loses its beauty
somehow, I find a small flame within,
that burns till it ignites a fire so high
that the demon disappears
back into the darkness.

Expectations

I am tired of being compared to
what a woman should be
she is so hard to live up to,
I just want to be.

Dear Mother

Mother,
look at me, I am drowning,
I am asking for your permission to swim to safety
that one more bite of food will not cause me to sink.
Mother,
please send me a signal
I need something more than
"You look fine sweetheart,"
"Your stomach just needs to be toned,
That's all,"
"You just need to stop eating so many carbs,
That's all,"
"Eat some fruits & vegetables,
That's all."
Mother,
please I need your reassurance
that I am worthy of self-love
that it is okay to not be perfect.
Mother,
please…

Thin as Paper

She carries her weight around
as if it were the emotions of the world.
Don't you see?
This isn't a vain attempt for beauty & control,
it's a fucking cry for the broken soul.

Vacant eyes lie in this emaciated body
tangled up in these repetitive words
line after line, follow the same path
useless gifts left to waste by the curbside.

There are days when all she wants to do is
embody the lines on the paper,
disappear & become nothing but
the words scribbled upon the page
living forever, thin as paper.

Beautiful Girls

Beautiful girls,
don't have scars that hide behind baggy clothes
they flaunt their flawless bodies.
Beautiful girls,
don't weight more than their boyfriends
they are dainty, have thigh gaps bigger than the London Bridge.
Beautiful girls,
don't have red blotchy acne upon their face
they wear make-up that covers their insecurities.
Beautiful girls,
it's so tiring trying to be a
beautiful girl.

A Letter to My Body

I am sorry I blamed you
stripped away your curves
like a sculptor, I chipped away
in search of perfection
destroyed what nourished me
& left nothing but dust & bones.

Braille

My scars read like Braille,
I cut through the old dead skin
to bring out the living,
like a burn victim
the old flesh tightens & suffocates me.
I must cut to be released,
to breathe again.

Relationship Goals

*The most important relationship
you will ever have
is the one with your
body and mind.
It is a lifelong relationship
that will follow you
to the grave.*

Hypocrites on the Forums

We've become
*		suicidal kids*
telling other
*		suicidal kids*
that suicide is not the answer.
*		We console,*
say encouraging words,
that it is all going to get better,
keep fighting through the pain,
*		life is worth living for.*
Strangers saying to strangers,
*		"Hun, I'm here if you need someone to talk to."*
But honestly, you're just as fucked up as
the person who is on the other end of the computer.

The sick trying to heal the sick.

In all actuality we are just feeding each other
*		bullshit,*
Because, you are just thinking the same
*		shit that they are thinking*
you can't convince someone else
*		that it's all going to be okay*
if you can't convince yourself.

Mindless Bodies

We have lost our appetites
too busy with our daily routine
to stop & pay attention
to our bodies.

Conquer each flesh
as if it isn't personal
the death & rebirth
of nothing
but lust.

Fucking away the pain.
Fucking away the time.

We are simply mindless bodies
falling into each other,
looking for meaning by
fucking empty souls
till our deaths catch up to us.

Malnourished

I get more nourishment from
what comes out of my mouth,
than what I put in it.

Control

Striving for
unattainable perfection
is your single-minded drive.
Years of
reaching,
dislocating,
tearing muscle from bone
hoping to attain a place in this world
you live in this bitter,
broken,
shell,
no longer able to mask the
imperfections
they stand out shining on the stage
bad thoughts,
spinning so bright that
they highlight the flaws
&
the small amount of control you had
slips through your boney fingers.

Parody of Emaciated Flesh

Bony toes
& hands,
emaciated fingers pointing
to a mirror image
of what she thinks
is a fat swollen knee.

Notches on the Belt

*Fingers trace down the spine
like notches on the belt I've tightened
there are scars upon these loose wrists.
Time stops,
the slow clicking of the heart
fades, as the body contorts
& disappears in ecstasy.
I roll off this high
as the mouth staves off
its basic convention
the skin decays
as we suck away
the lives we would've
had if we hadn't dissolved
into this disease.*

I Can't Get No Satisfaction

I don't know why it has
become so hard to breathe,
as if the air has become still
& my lungs are no longer satisfied
with the air filing its emptiness.

Mothers and Daughters

Mother,
I don't blame you
I'm just sorry that
we have learned to place
all our self-worth in our
beauty and our bodies
for it is fleeting &
we are so much more.

I Don't Want a Daughter

I don't want a daughter.

I'm scared that my ego will weight her down
we spend our lives competing against each other
I don't want a daughter to grow up
in a world where she must fight against the men who
push her down to her knees &
the women who keep her there.
'It's her place' they say.

In high school we compete for looks,
Who is the prettiest?
Who is the skinniest?
Who has the best tits?

We are our own worst enemies
we use our bodies to survive,
a bit more cleavage to
get free drinks with a side of obligation
to the men who wait at bar
who stare like starving dogs at the last piece of meat.

I don't want a daughter.

Awful Pretenses

I'm an awful wreck
I've become numb, keeping up with pretenses
It's exhausting
I'm trying to keep contact with the outside world
instead I just tend to stare the day away.
The sun has set the day has gone,
it's time for you to go home now,
the day is over, and everyone has gone home.

Decay

*Your mouth may be pretty
but your words are ugly.*

Grocery Store on the Corner of Main and 3rd

I am just starting to eat again
when I'm standing in line
to get my groceries &
Cosmo, US Weekly & People Magazine
are all yelling at me
to lose that last bit of body fat
before swimsuit season,
that I must find some
new way of pleasing men
or my place will be filled
with someone who is
prettier & skinnier than I.
They call after me,
"Mam, you have lost your place in line!"

15 years

It's been Fifteen years that I've been
dealing with an eating disorder
what they don't tell you is you never fully recover.
I still hear her in the back of my mind
quietly counting the calories of every meal I eat
scrutinizing every pound of flesh.

When I was in high school
I was the "go to girl" for advice on how to lose weight.
"What are your tips & tricks?"

I carry their weight.

My friends thought it was great because,
I can recall the nutritionist facts
in their regular McDonalds meal,
like I'm the rain man of fucking calories.
They don't realize that I would trade
my poetry,
give up all my writings,
if it meant I could recondition myself to never
see that fat girl in the mirror again.

Fifteen years,
I have been hunched over computer screens
secretly coveting bodies thinner than mine
hitting the like button,
the silent follower.
my profile states,
"Not Pro Ana! If you are Pro Ana do not follow me."
I am not the solution to your problem

I am the cause.

Fifteen years,
I claim I am in remission because I feel I am
too fat to say that I am not.

Half

I'm half as graceful
as I seem,
I'm half as confident
as I'll ever let you see,
I'm easy on the eyes yet,
easy to forget.

I'm half as beautiful
as you think,
I'm half as kind
as you've been led to believe.
I'm easy on the eyes yet,
easy to forget.

I'm half as happy
as I'll ever be,
I'm half as loved
as I'll ever need,
but God please don't let me
hear those words again,
cause I'm easy on the eyes yet,
so damn easy to forget.

Perfect Imperfections

When we look down at our bodies, we
pick apart each flaw
compare how we see ourselves in the mirror
to how others us.
We focus on all the imperfections
instead of what makes us unique.
How far my stomach juts out doesn't matter
my body tells beautiful stories of what I have been through.
When I look down, I no longer focus on weight.
I see the scars of a warrior, a survivor,
the stretch marks & cellulite of a woman who has grown
who has lived.
I see hair upon my legs, my pits, between my thighs.
My body tells a story & it's fucking amazing.

What is your story?

Mature

Clear thoughts, time &
a touch of a maturity
you realize that your self-destructive nature
does nothing but hurt others around you.

Part III

The Blood
I thought if I wrote it down
That it would make more sense
That the blood spilled would clean itself up
And I could go back to being the Ragdoll

I am not Adam's Eve

Am I less than you
because God plucked your stem
& turned it into my flower?

10 years

*After ten years the word rape does not feel like it belongs to me. I
trusted a man who used my naivety against me. I spent four months
trapped in his maliciousness, thinking that real love meant bruised
hips & ultimatums.
Back then girls didn't really bring up the subject of rape like they do
now & if they did, no one ever believed them.
Things have changed a lot.
We still have a lot to change.
That's not to say that if I would have said something that my
parents or someone wouldn't have believed me.
They would have.
But I didn't believe it. So how could they.*

Blank Pages

I don't know who I am anymore,
I've lost touch with my soul
the reality I once lived in.
I am numb.
I've written this
between
blank pages,
too afraid
for this to be the first entry
in this book.

Hands

I am in love with
his hands,
beautiful & callused,
waiting to press against my flesh,
touch my lips,
quiet me
into submission.

Misunderstood

How magnificently cunning you are
the devil in the details
with each sentence you find
another fork at the road
take the wrong turn
& blame me for poor directions.

Bukowski

He once told me
I smoked cigarettes like
it was crack & probably
fucked the way he imagined
Bukowski would've,
hard & careless.

Good Intentions

I wanted the kind of love
that shook you
with a right hook
back hand
punish me then promise me
you'll pave our way to Hell with
your good intentions.

The Muse

Thoughts pass through me
eager to be discussed
but the words fall short & hit my tongue
then bounce back into my throat
every time I turn around someone has stolen
the words right from under my tongue.
How many times have callused fingered men
looked for meaning in this empty soul?
They call me their muse
but in the end
I am left wordless.

Play-Doe

*I am made of play-doe
the world molds me into
what they want.*

*Look,
she's a lion.
Look,
now she's a lamb.*

Cancer

You are cancer
Smoke that suffocates
Stifling my words
You are an invisible illness
The quiet killer
Silencing me
While I smile politely
You are the bruise hidden
In my thigh
The painful reminder that
I should know my place.
You might be cancer
But I am the fucking radiation
Fighting back
To put you right in your place.

Dancing with the Devil

I made love to the devil,
as we tossed between the blue flames
I fell upon his hellish coals,
& saw his cold eyes
lusting for more beneath my warm flesh.

Lost Sheets

I lost myself last night
somewhere between
the loose sheets
I woke up naked,
numb & red eyed
& I can't seem to remember
what I lost to begin with.

Broken Rag Doll

He calls me his little doll
his little toy that he can dominate
I have maintained control for so many years
that I want to give in so badly
I want to let go
let the monster in.

He calls me his little doll
as he paints me like his shadows
forever trapped in his canvas
of lies.

He calls me his little rag doll,
while he drags me through the mud
then leaves me broken upon his shelf.

One More

*One more sip.
It's all right
now,
drink it down,
as demons fly,
from the mouth
past demon lips,
down her throat,
while her body screams
let the monsters grow.*

*It's just another night
she'll look for blissful thoughts,
at the bottom of the bottle,
she'll lose herself in demon eyes,
just before dusk comes undone.*

Plot Twist

You are not alone.
You are not just another statistic.
You are not another plot twist to make someone else's story
interesting. Our experiences good & bad make us
who we are, but it does not mean they control you.
Do not hide for fear that others will believe you are broken.
Your story isn't a plot twist.
Your story is a fucking revolution.
& you will be silenced no longer.

Double Standards

Double standards
that's the way this world is
I am told that I must sit back and accept
that men will be forever celebrated for their conquests
over their loss of innocence
& women will be stoned.
The sluts who rally against
the men who wouldn't take their
No for an answer.

The Sentencing of the Stanford Rapist

*"You didn't know me
but you have been inside me" – Stanford Survivor*

*Your sentence might have been shortened for fear
of what impact that it might have on
your future?
Yet, no one thought of my fellow sister's future?
The impact on
her skin
her sex
her memories
forever tainted
her sentence will be far greater than what
any judge could ever sentence you.*

Bad Men

Bad men
don't look like the strangers
lurking in dark alleyways
they are the men you thought
you loved.
They kiss your mouth gently &
whisper all the good intentions they are paving
to Hell.

Bad men,
look beautiful
when they write you poetry
& seduce you with words.
They find that one piece of jewelry
you've coveted &
choke you with it.

Bad men,
control you
till you no longer remember who you were
only who they want you to be
& you mourn the strong, confident woman
you could have been.

In Case He Told You Something Different

What you wear doesn't matter
it does nothing to invite unwanted guests
they are just clothes.

Sympathy for the Devil

We died upon decaying beds,
        blood stained from the last victim.
I
burned for him
with blissful naiveté
but knew not of the consequence.
I
fell to his prey,
the cunning mate
waiting to conquer the body
bruise the soul.
I
sympathized with the aggressor
but could only blame the act
not the vessel.

Black and Blue

*I let him abuse me for months
because I thought love meant
having bruised hips
shut lips.*

Monsters

*Nothing fills
    the vile
        gash
            between
                my thighs
                in the night
            I fuck the
        monsters in the
shadows of
                my thighs.*

Comatose but Audible

She is terrified of his silence.
The meaning behind
deaf ears.
She prays for strength to endure his
quivering lips and pulsating thighs.
With a spiteful tongue,
she spits his seeds out
just like his lies.
He lays her out upon his bed,
"You're such a coward," she cries
"Look into my eyes and rape my body dry."

My Body Must Remember

I starve my body
in hopes it would let me forget
his malicious tongue
against bruised hips.
The mind tends to cover the scars
the body can never return.
I will not remember…
Instead I will wear my life upon my body
let it wither till I can no longer see his
cunning face above mine.
If my mind cannot remember
than my body must.

Shhhhh…. This is not the time or the place for that non-sense

The first man I met in college
raped me as soon as I let my guard down
words were the only way I could cope
yet my story was "too serious"
for our college level classes.

I placed it in a drawer
locked & threw away the key
no one wants to sit so uncomfortable
in their privileged seats
best not raise the issue
it's just a bit too sensitive &
it was probably her fault anyway.

Silent No More

I live a quiet life,
though my thoughts are loud as hell
the world has quieted me
I want to say what I'm too afraid to say
but my words are stifled
they get caught in my throat
by men who choke them down
years of being conditioned to be silent.

I am silent no more.

Me Too

Today I heard the cry of women
screaming no
placing stop signs on the corners
of their home
You are trespassing

Today I heard the cry of women
defending themselves
taking the stand
Judge, I did not provoke him
He broke into my home
There is no more to the story
there is no justifying why

Today I heard the cry of women.
Believe us
We cannot hold the guilt of men
inside our small bodies

We will rise
we will scream our battle cry &
reclaim our bodies.

Meteors

What do we do
when the angels have fallen from the sky?
I will no longer wish upon
fallen stars
for they leave craters
as wide as my aspirations.

Phoenix

He did not take the fire
that burns in my blood
a phoenix has risen from
the ashes in my stead,
I am here & he will
no longer snuff out my flame.

The Wrath of Persephone

Don't just burry the pain
let it move through you
let the grief destroy the shackles
that once held you down
& let your wrath sing upon the world
for it is beautiful.

Part IV

The Soul

I am not an empty vessel

I am filled with anger

Spite

& a light that will drown out the darkness

A Shot of Whiskey and a Shovel

You can't fix the pain
but you can dig a grave for it.

Recipe for the Broken

You must give up the darkness
let it bleed out into the ink
& think of it no more.

Civil War

*"I love you," will start a revolution
        a civil war
                between my defenses and the soul.*

Little Battles

I fight battles every day
little ones in hope that I will
win the war.
I am worthy of this flesh
I am worthy of my lover's flesh
he might have taken away my virtue
but he will not haunt my body.

Feminist Unleashed

Somewhere along the way
someone told me to quiet my voice,
to be the watcher in the room
instead of the singer,
to be embarrassed by the
loudmouth,
thick girl,
in your face,
telling you ideas, you don't want to accept
today, my voice is no longer quiet.

Equality

You expedite sins
like overdue rent
tell the minister to
check his facts
Adam and Eve ate
the same piece of fruit
as if she forced the seeds down his throat.
We are equal,
My brother,
My husband,
My father,
We all sin the same.

Baggage

There are humans
in this world with baggage
deep as an old lady's handbag,
people who with
scars upon their bodies
scars within their souls
so deep they are scared that
the wounds will never heal.
But you are not alone
& your scars will fade
into beautiful moonlit stars.

Scars Pt II

Time mends the bleeding heart
& leaves nothing but a faint
scar upon your chest
to remind you of the
love that was placed there.

Sunburn

Too much time spent
pealing back dead skin
from sunburnt skin
searching for someone new
underneath the sun.

I'm my own Swayze

Nobody puts baby in the corner
this baby speaks the fuck up & tells
the man exactly where she wants to sit.

Gut Shot

I know that my voice
isn't as strong as the words
that I write but
they pack a powerful punch to your gut.
They will make you second guess
this small framed girl
who stutters when nervous
& stops
mid
sentence
but you will remember my words.

Ashamed

I have been ashamed for too long
scared that my lists of diagnosis and problems
have become too much of a burden for others to bare
phrases like she's hypochondriac,
looking for attention,
someone to pity her,
makes me push away the need to share
how I am feeling,
when I am hurting
& I all I need is someone to listen to me,
not to pity me,
because I will no longer be ashamed.

Healthy Dreams

My eyes feel like sinkholes
their weight is so heavy it
buries into my head
weighs down my mind
like sandbags
brain filled with
dirt & dust & sleep.
Rest &
let dreams of a healthy tomorrow
be true.

Tree of Life

This body is full of beauty
lush growth, overgrown
waiting to spread love
upon the earth
even after death.

To All Disabled Warriors

We are fighters
our illness does not define us
it gives us strength
that others do not have
beauty that shines through darkness
because we are capable of
moving mountains with our hearts.

Guilt Free

*You deserve
all the Netflix, Oreos,
& late night
guilt free binges.*

Healthy Relationships

Forgive me, my lover
I have taken your gentle touch for granted
I have mistaken it for backhanded lovers
I flinch at your sweet kisses
for they are not the teeth of hungry men.
Forgive me, my lover
for you are not them.

Lotus Refrain

Tonight, I will reclaim my body
my fruit will no longer
be rotten from his seeds
tonight, I will raise my voice
& sing into the night.

The Last Waltz

The shadows creep as
dark spirits come up to catch her
darkness engulfs her
clinging to her hips.

She waltzes with the specters,
feet gracefully tracing
outlines of the past.

She dances as she lets go of the memories.

She throws herself upon the stage
her body contorts as
she moves to the rhythm
waiting for redemption between beats.

She dances as she lets go of the pain.
She dances till the shadows fade
& become beautiful streams of light.

Chaotic Melody & Minor Keys

For three years, I set up camp, built up walls
with only blame to keep me company
anger filled my body like a disease
I let myself believe that I deserved
chaotic melodies,
minor keys filled with bruises.

When I finally sang again
I was hesitant of a man's gentle touch
a sweet release,
the take down brick by brick
instead of a violent crash.

Gardens

Your tears give birth
To a life you thought
You never could have
Let go of the pain &
Let the flowers grow.

10 Minute Intervals

You deserve a shelf of trophies
for every moment you get through.
Sometimes you must break life up
into 10-minute intervals
just to get through the day.

Saving Grace

We look for a man to save.
We look for a man to save us.
When we look for nothing at all,
We find that we save ourselves.

It's Okay to Not Be Okay

Healing is not linear
It is as chaotic and irregular
As a heart attack.